GW00776045

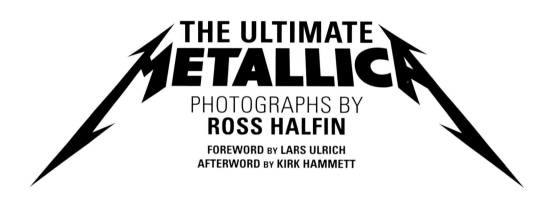

THE ULTIMATE
METALLICA

PHOTOGRAPHS BY
ROSS HALFIN

FOREWORD BY **LARS ULRICH**
AFTERWORD BY **KIRK HAMMETT**

CHRONICLE BOOKS

SAN FRANCISCO

Library of Congress Cataloging-in-Publication Data available.
ISBN: 978-0-8118-7505-9

Manufactured in China

Art Direction & Design by Tom Jermann / t42design

10 9 8 7 6 5 4 3 2 1

Chronicle Books LLC
680 Second Street
San Francisco, CA 94107
www.chroniclebooks.com

Note

As Lars has written such a great intro (and boys and girls he really has) . . .
I feel I should explain a bit about the sayings of mine that he still retains . . .

PFL: Protruding Forehead Look, as in anyone losing their hair, or in the case
of Lars and me, "a large forehead."

Cutting Into My Jack Time: This one came from Bonham's singer Daniel
McMaster, who told me to hurry up as I was CUTTING INTO THEIR JACK TIME!

NF: Trust me you don't want to know! It started with the drawing on the
inner bag of . . . *And Justice for All.*

Grumble: As in a person of the female variety . . . as in "where's the Grumble?"

Easy Nick and *I Told You:* These come from Iron Maiden drummer Nicko
McBrain, who on the Iron Maiden Powerslave Tour would have tantrums
like a three-year-old child all day, every day. Nicko would on many occasions
scream at various people in hotels and airports "I TOLD YOU" . . . followed
by "DO YOU KNOW WHO I AM?". . . Iron Maiden played (I think) 114 shows
on that tour, and Nicko changed rooms at least 98 times. Once he came
down screaming "WHO PUT ME IN THAT ROOM? THE COLOR OF THE
WALLPAPER'S MAKING ME SICK." . . . So anyone who complains or raises
their voice is told "Easy, Nick" . . . I even to this day call all children "Nick"
after Nicko.

There's even a few more, but I'll spare you. Ask Lars . . .

– R.H.

ACKNOWLEDGMENTS

This book would not be possible without a few big thank-yous:

Tom Jermann for the idea
Lars Ulrich, Kirk Hammett, and Peter Mensch for putting pen to laptop
Tony DiCioccio for reining in the copy
Noriaki "Nori Burger" Watanabe for sorting out my files
and helping select the photos
Kazuyo Horie for being there
Phil Lemon for the black-and-white printing
Steffan Chirazi for his enthusiasm and help

I sincerely hope you like this book.

I started shooting Metallica with Olympus OM-2 cameras. I had two which were light and easy to use. The downside was they broke quite easily. I switched to Nikon F3s when Metallica did their first Japanese tour in 1987. I bought them the day before I left, got to Japan, and realized I had no idea how to use them, so I just figured it out through trial and error. I also used a Mamiya 6×7 large-format camera. Now I use a Nikon D3S.

I've used and use these Nikkor lenses:
105mm
85mm
70–200mm
14mm
16mm
50mm
24–70mm
My most used, and favorite, lens is the 85mm.

As this is a list of work stuff, I should thank my assistants from the Metallica years: Andrew Clatworthy—who once drank a pint of Kirk's urine, which, in all fairness, Kirk gave to him; Rory Moles, Steve Crise, Laurance Baker, Nigel Case, Scarlet Page (who thought they were all vile), Noriaki "General Noriega" Watanabe—and the longest suffering, Kazuyo Horie (who loves them all).

FOREWORD BY LARS ULRICH

Ross Halfin.

" . . . cuz he's mellowed out!!"

We'll come back to that.

Ross asked me to write the intro for this, the 147th installment in the "Another Useless Book of Metallica Photos That You Don't Really Need/Want" (he may have retitled it by now!!) and as I'm sitting here trying to figure out what the fuck to write, it just dawned on me that the previous 146 installments all have intros written by various members of the band, in some cheap attempt to legitimize them, to make you, the 'Tallica fanatic, feel that this, the next waste of space in your library, has a legit value somewhere north of toilet paper.

The last time I did this pointless intro exercise was in the spring of 1996, when 'Tallica and Ross were about to be taking a much-needed break from each other after 12 years of—eh—working together. Honestly, we had run out of white walls to stand in front of, run out of tourist monuments to be used as background scenery in far-off exotic locations, run out of things to say to each other, run out of insults to throw at each other. The creative well was, well . . . dry. Our relationship remained on hiatus for over a decade. The astute and observant of you may notice a somewhat large gap in the timeline of photos in this here book, probably most evident in the hair department, or perhaps that should read "lack-of-hair" department. There were a few semi-courteous social encounters here and there over the years, but nothing inspiring, nothing spark igniting. "Why did we start using Ross again," I hear myself ask Tony DiCioccio, feeling somewhat puzzled and bewildered on a recent April evening as I try to recall . . . "Cuz you started talking to him again." "Why did I start talking to him again?" "Cuz he's mellowed out!!" Well, that sounds as reasonable as anything I can remember three years later on, so. . . . Then more or less, just like that, we picked it back up again in the summer of 2007 in Lisbon, Portugal, where after a couple of good shoot days and one long debaucherous night involving shots of a different kind and lots of catching up, it effortlessly fell back into place. The love is back. Alright, let's not go that far . . . the appreciation??? Yes, we can use that one. The appreciation is back.

Ross Halfin is an enigma. A contradiction. An artist. An effortless master of his niche. A rock 'n' roll photographer. Mostly hard rock, mostly live. An enigma because he doesn't really seem to do all that much except click away. And the results of that effortless clicking away often seem so much grander than I anticipate. So much more intense, spectacular, and often more defining than expected. When I notice him lurking around the stage and I have a momentary awareness of his presence, it just doesn't seem like he does all that much. But of course, as all great masters of their domain, he has his thing down. Way down. And his thing is being not only in the right place at the right time, but at the right angle, with the right perspective, the right line of sight, etc. That's why he is an enigma to me. Because I often can't correlate the results with such effortlessness.

Ross Halfin has also been a big part of my life. He's photographed more of it than not. He's inspired parts of my life. Woah!!! Time out. How about influenced? That's better. He somehow, at a very young age when we were green and gullible, helped shape our outlook on the rock 'n' roll life. He had a certain aloof relationship with his work, with the people around him that kept him from being too mesmerized with his subjects, prevented him from being star-struck that moved him closer, closer in. Often this aloofness would surface as a barrage of insults, put-downs, and wind-ups, which, especially to the young American subjects who were less schooled in the "high wire act" of British humor/sarcasm/irony, would often leave Mr. Halfin, to put it mildly, one of the least liked men in rock 'n' roll. But it did somehow keep his feet planted firmly on the ground and, in some peculiar way, rubbed off on the rest of us. It was as if making fun of the all-around ridiculousness, the rock star element of the world we inhabited, prevented us all from getting too caught up in its web, its traps, and the shortfalls that came in believing in the elements of grandeur, invincibility, and the lack of mortality. I do believe that our exposure to the English ways, especially in the early years, helped us tremendously over time, and in some way you could argue that the small army of English tour managers, assistants, minders, and writers that hovered around us over the years and kept us in line had Ross Halfin as their spiritual leader.

I also love Ross Halfin. I love the fact he takes my picture. I love the fact that the guy who took all those iconic pictures of the people that most influenced me during my most impressionable years now takes my picture. By the way, those people being Ritchie Blackmore, Steve Harris, Lemmy, Phil Lynott, the list goes on . . . set your watches to 1978 onwards. Think *Sounds*, think *Kerrang!* Think an open, receptive, enthusiastic young Danish kid following Ross's escapades on a weekly basis across the globe, with a relentless thirst to be there with him on his next adventure. That guy now takes my picture and I fuckin' love it. Actually, he doesn't just take my picture on stage, he hovers, hangs out, gets in my face, invades my zone, pushes me to another level. . . . I bet that over the years he has spent more time within three feet of me being spit and sweated on than any of the other cats in the band, or Flemming, my tech, for that matter. This probably is Ross Halfin's strongest attribute. He just gets right the fuck in there, like I said before, "closer in," more so than anyone else. Every drop of sweat, every molecule of saliva, every out-of-place nose hair, it all gets captured cuz he's just fucking there. And that "just fucking there" is who he is. His personality, his reason for being, his way. And that's why you not only have to tolerate his way and accept his way, but deep down inside, at gunpoint, you will have to admit to even *liking* his way. Admit to understanding it and, dare I say, loving it. Because the pictures, or photographs as some prefer, are unlike anybody else's, closer in, more invasive, just . . . more.

Ross Halfin has introduced certain phrases into my vocabulary that I still can't rid myself of saying, some of them more than 20 years after they were first uttered in some random, impulsive, borderline Tourette's-like way, over and over again until you were pulling your hair out. Come to think of it, I just realized that the reason most of us have so little hair left may be directly linked to the amount of time we've spent in the vicinity of Ross Halfin, on and off over the last 30 years. It explains a lot, actually. Hang on . . . back to the phrases: I still occasionally find myself uttering "Easy Nick!!!" for no fuckin' reason whatsoever. Ross, who the fuck is Nick?? And why do I still walk around 20 years later and call out his name?? The list unfortunately goes on. "PFL"???? "Grumble"??? "This is cutting into my Jack time!!" "I told you!!!" "NF" (you definitely don't wanna go there!!). Maybe there is a Ross Halfin dictionary in the future, instead of these recycled photo books???!!!

When I think of Metallica it's impossible not to be somewhat influenced by Ross's pictures. Over the years I have had a tendency to correlate events and happenings in the Metallica timeline with cerebral snapshots, visual memories, and other mile markers I have flagged along the way. Now let's be honest, a good portion of those are obviously photographs, and a good portion of those photographs are obviously Ross Halfin's. For better or for worse, whether it involves silver face paint, Chinese food, the fog of the Marin Headlands, the Sydney Opera House, the desert in Arizona, the sidewalks of North Hollywood, or various sweat, spit, and blood infused rock 'n' roll stages all over the world, Ross Halfin's mark is often imprinted when I access the Metallica memory bank, located deep in the bowels of my thick Danish skull.

Back to ". . . cuz he's mellowed out!!"

Ross Halfin used to be out of his mind. And I mean this in the most positive of ways. Take it from somebody who is also out of his mind. I'm out of my mind enough to admit that the paragraphs that best describe his out-of-his-mindness were written in a hotel room in New York City in the spring of 1996, "the last time I did this pointless intro exercise." Fourteen years later, no matter how I slice and dice it, I think it's best to simply reprint two paragraphs from the last intro to illustrate what I'm talking about. Here goes . . .

". . . Of any person I have encountered in the music business in the last fifteen years who excels in his/her particular field, Ross Halfin can be a pain in the ass like no other. 'The fucken thing has fallen out!!' After traveling to the farthest outpost of whatever corner of the world we happen to be in, trekking 45 minutes (uphill!?), waiting for an hour in the scorching heat for the lights to be set up, realizing it's your only day off for a week, and then

being told to hold your fucken pose for yet another hour, after Ross realizes that the previous hour's work was shot at the wrong film speed and then . . . 'The fucken thing has fallen out!' . . . The little wire connecting the whatever to the other whatever has now blown halfway across the prairie and you just wanna fucken go 'AAAAARRRRRGGGGGHHHHH!!!! Fuck!!!' But instead Ross beats you to it, insults the shit out of you for potentially pulling a rock star head trip and being a whining spoilt brat and continuously riding the shit out of you for the following hour, while periodically pulling his pants down, farting the most obnoxious-sounding farts this side of Blazing Saddles *while phrases like 'Chin up' get uttered about 614 times too many. . . . (I'm glad I finally got that out of my system!!) The man is very lucky he hasn't gotten his head bashed in a few times, considering I know we are even more tolerant than most of his other 'victims'!!*

"But what is it people say, 'You have to bleed for your art,' and God knows he does that!! I have seen Ross push the boundaries of what would be considered sane over the last few years and, once again, God only knows that together we have pushed rock photography to a level of . . . shall we say . . . slightly OT fucken T! Part of the reason I think we have worked so well together is because deep down inside, me and the man are not that different from each other in terms of determination and tenacity, and that will get you into a few slightly different situations. . . . A few that spring to mind . . . Alaskan glaciers with 'Nam flashback 'copter pilots, riverboats in Bangkok, mad Hungarians, and even madder Hungarian police escorts, 2 A.M. drunker-than-shit, post-gig field shots in Germany, even drunker sessions in the gutter outside my house in El Cerrito, taking roughly 7000 shots of us in front of the opera house in Sydney over the span of three days ('Are you sure we got it??!!'), not to mention things like silly spray-painted silver faces (??), Chinese food in all orifices, Arizona 4 A.M. desert shots, gakked-out sessions on the beach in Brazil, Japanese marriage intrusions, Heinekens in Red Square in Moscow, being insulted by a pair of ten-year-olds in London ('Oi, Dickhead! Your mother's a penis!?') . . . Jeez, I am starting to get all misty-eyed here, this is half my fucken life. . . ."

And he still is out of his mind. Still meant in the most positive of ways of course. But I will agree with Tony DiCioccio. He has mellowed out. To be fair, I've also mellowed out quite a bit. Maybe that's why the working relationship is back on track. Still working. What's the point of all this mellowing out business? . . . Yes! . . . I'm almost done! . . . You will get to these fucking pictures momentarily, most of which you've already seen, remember? The point is that this book would be quite a bit shorter if it wasn't for the mellowing out. Or it would abruptly end with the live pictures from the *Load* era tour, circa fall 1996. Because as you can see, there is quite a generous helping of new stuff, new photos, new vibes that document the further, new improved shenanigans of 'Tallica and they are there because the dynamic has once again found a way to function . . . Hell, maybe it even functions better than it used to, this Halfin-'Tallica relationship. And the mellowing out of not just Ross Halfin, but all the other guilty parties, may be the primary reason, the key factor. Come to think of it, this may also be the reason Metallica functions better than ever. Who the fuck knows, but it's a nice theory, don't you think?

INTRODUCTION BY PETER MENSCH

What you are about to read, or more likely just look at, is a pictorial history of one man, his camera, and a band. But, it's more than that. It's actually an overview of a pure distinct color in the rainbow that is rock music. And as such, you need to understand some of the background.

I met Ross Halfin around 1980, maybe even before, in the fall of 1979. England had, as England does every so often, spawned a new genre of music titled "The New Wave of British Heavy Metal" or something like that. I was living in the U.K. and so for me it was just "The New Wave of Heavy Metal," because frankly, the old wave was mostly missing in action. America was into punk (having followed the U.K. punk movement), and we metal fans were searching. So on came Maiden, Leppard, Saxon, Diamondhead, etc., and with them came new support personnel. New managers, promoters, agents, record companies, and Ross Halfin.

Ross was (and still is) an odd fellow. He came with an attitude and a chip on his shoulder bigger than Ben Nevis, which meant he fit in perfectly with all of these bands and their managers and publicists. He, like the rest of us, just didn't fit in with the previous legendary photographers, none of whom would deign to shoot these bands. Probably, like the rest of us who either wanted to be in a legendary band or manage a legendary band, Ross wanted to photograph legendary bands. So we all set out to make those new British HM bands into legends. And, with Maiden and Leppard, we succeeded to a point.

But it was with the rise of Metallica and what they represented that we all succeeded beyond our wildest dreams.

Besides being ornery and artistically difficult, Ross is also very smart and perceptive, which meant he was going to be perfect for Lars Ulrich. Besides being an excellent drummer and co-writer of all of Metallica's music, Lars is also the "business head" in the band and would therefore be the go-to guy for things like suggesting a new photographer. As far as I was concerned, I only wanted "new-school" guys taking pictures of my new-school bands—mostly because the old schoolers shat on all of our heads, but also because I wanted a fresh look. I knew Ross would match up with Lars perfectly and we would get results. And results we got. In spades.

If you wanted a band shot, you got a distinctive one. If you wanted Ross in the pit, you would get great shots because the band knew and trusted Ross. If you wanted something distinct—a different angle, whatever—Ross would get into the spirit of things and all of a sudden would be hanging from a lighting truss.

Ross knows the language of Metallica. He's known it since day one. He could talk obscure English bands with them or talk about stories of Zeppelin or The Who. He got Lars perfectly (maybe one day the "swelling of" T-shirt will see the light of day). He understood the elemental power of James Hetfield, the grace and spirituality of Kirk Hammett, and the doggedness of Jason Newsted.

Years later, Ross would be estranged from Metallica for stupid reasons that I was never sure of. It bothered me for a while, but I had other fish to fry. Finally, I (and maybe others) insisted that we repair the rift and get back to what we should have been doing all the time. Maybe it was the arrival of Robert Trujillo (one of the all-time great guys and great bassists) or everybody just relaxing, but Ross is back, and back with a vengeance.

I've known Ross for 30 years. He hasn't changed much and probably neither have I. Maybe we've both mellowed a bit, but don't go looking for it. We've just dropped the intensity from 11 to 10.5. I owe him in far too many ways to list, but I will tell you that his work with Metallica is even better than I could have imagined it when I put them together. And for that, I will always be grateful.

Peter Mensch is the co-owner and founder (with Cliff Burnstein) of the management company Q Prime, which has worked with Metallica since 1984.

RANDOM THOUGHTS ON METALLICA BY ROSS HALFIN

In truth, I first shot Metallica only because of the persistence of their manager, Peter Mensch. A few journalists had already warned me that Lars was trying to get in touch, purely on the basis that I'd shot all of Iron Maiden's photos, but I'd been avoiding him for a couple of months. At the time, Lars had become somewhat infamous for photo shoots in magazines in which he'd be holding flaming drumsticks or pulling wet plastic over his face while looking . . . stupid; well, stupid is the wrong word, perhaps, but he certainly looked "Danish," given that most of my youthful impressions of Danes involved them being carried off planes after drinking too much and being loaded into ambulances on the runway.

Anyway, I was in Seattle shooting Queensryche in November 1984 when Mensch phoned me. I still remember his exact words: "Stop being an ASSHOLE and go and shoot my new band. . . ."

So off I went.

At the time Metallica, or maybe it was just James and Lars, lived in a house together in El Cerrito. The house had lots of Motörhead posters on the walls and one by me of Michael Schenker—which endeared me to Kirk. My original idea for the photoshoot was to reference the Rolling Stones' *Beggars Banquet* album cover, as frankly I couldn't think of anything else to do with them. Sadly, there was no stuffed venison or wild boar in sunny Oakland, so I had to make do with Chinese takeaway and bottles of Smirnoff vodka. Actually, we had to order two takeaways, as the first lot that arrived the band ate. . . . Then I looked at Lars and thought, "I know, let's spray him silver with a metal cake. . . ." I still have no idea where the cake—or the nuts and bolts we put in it—came from. To this day, I think it's possibly one of the worst photos I have ever taken, but look, it seemed like a really good idea in 1984. I cringe now thinking about it. . . . However, it did end up being the shot used for the band's very first magazine cover in the U.K. When Paul Brannigan was working for that magazine he told me that whenever a band was being difficult and precious about photo shoots he'd say, "If Lars Ulrich can spray himself silver . . ." Kinda says it all in the world of photography.

The next time I shot them was in February '85 in New York. I was there with Iron Maiden—we were on our way home from Rock in Rio—and Metallica were in the city too. We did photos on the aircraft carrier in the Hudson River. It was so cold that I gave up after a while. Like all bands, they looked awkward and unsure at the start, in fact they looked exactly like fans . . . which is exactly what they were.

Somewhere in here I started to go on tour with them. It was easy in the sense that they were enthusiastic and they understood the reason behind doing photos. We would shoot everywhere, which would be nice now except that we'd never be left alone, and as Lars carries five phones you wouldn't know which one to call him on. But after a while they started to evolve and have their own look. The Metallica look—kind of like Clint Eastwood in *The Good, The Bad, and The Ugly,* a defiant "Do not mess with us" sort of thing—came together after I stopped them messing around.

I mean, they did mess around, but the photographer has to have control and respect, and they respected what I did. Plus they started to get my slightly evil sense of humor. . . .

At the time Cliff and James both had disdain for any other band that was not "cool" and by that they meant not METAL. They may laugh now but back then they were serious . . . they thought that most of the '80s bands (remember, hair metal was in) were poseurs and should be killed . . . preferably slowly. James even had a guitar with a KILL BON JOVI sticker on the back of it, which upset Jon Bon Jovi so much he got his manager to call up Q Prime (Metallica's management) to ask James not to use it in when they played New Jersey—this really is true.

The main crux of touring with them was having a good time. When they played the Palladium in LA in March '85 with Adam Bomb and Armored Saint—who were headlining their big hometown show—Lars, James, and Kirk made me tell Cliff that Black Sabbath's Geezer Butler, his hero, was at the show. Cliff played his bass solo "Anesthesia" trembling. Geezer, of course, wasn't there. . . . This show was the only time I've ever seen a band annihilate a headliner: Armored Saint just could not follow them. I have a vivid memory of James doing a backflip into the audience at the end of the show.

I shot them again at their house in El Cerrito in July '85. After shooting them in their living room as a group, all four of them sitting on the couch, we drove off (I think in Cliff's truck) to the Golden Gate Bridge, where I figured I'd get the shot overlooking the Bay. However, I hadn't counted on the fog. . . . These shots ended up on the *Master of Puppets* album.

I also remember spending a freezing day with them in Copenhagen during the recording of *Master of Puppets*. They carried my camera gear for about half a mile across a snowy, frozen soccer field only for us to realize that there was a gate about five feet away from the studio they were in. I also shot photos of them in the studio; in hindsight I wish I'd shot more. Then again, you always look back at things and think you could have done better.

When *Master of Puppets* was released they went out on the road in America, supporting Ozzy Osbourne in arenas. I went on tour with them in the spring of '86 to such exotic locations as Des Moines (we were there for three whole days), Minneapolis, and Pine Knob—yes, there really is a place called Pine Knob, and The Agora in Chicago, where I shot them on the stairwell (photos that I still really like) and in the middle of a pile of rubbish, I kid you not.

One time in LA, Lars was determined that I would take him to Nikki Sixx's porno party: after drinking sake all night in a sushi bar we drove around Bel Air and Lars said sarcastically to my date, who was speeding, "Why don't you go a bit faster?" As he said this we whacked the curb, spun 'round in the road, hit the opposite curb, and somersaulted, landing upside down, half in the road and half in someone's garden. I remember it all seemed to happen in slow motion. I looked around the car and everyone was okay. We crawled out the window with my date screaming "My car!" as it was going up in flames. Three police cars arrived. I'm thinking, "Oh shit . . . we're wasted. . . ." They handcuffed and carted my date off to jail, and the sergeant looked at Lars and me and said, "I have scraped people off this corner. There is not a mark on any of you. Remember this: God is watching you." He then ordered us a couple of cabs. Lars rang me at 6 A.M. saying, "Did that really happen?"

I actually have Lars to thank for my love life. While with Iron Maiden in Tel Aviv, I was approached by a girl in a club. "You're Lars Ulrich!" she gasped, ignoring Steve Harris (bassist for Iron Maiden), who was standing beside me. "Is it really you?" . . . "Yes, it's really me . . . ." She even asked me for an autograph when she left the following morning. I've been told hundreds of times that I look like Lars: let's get this clear, I don't . . . Lars looks like me.

Another time, on a flight to Hungary, after drinking pints—like you do when you are young and stupid—at Heathrow (there are photos of this), Kirk and I sat in our seats and examined our penises (don't ask me why!). The purser shouted, "Put those away or I'll have you both arrested." Metallica, in an '80s boys' own way, were a lot of moronic *fun*. It was a sort of club with no membership that you joined. They respected me and I respected them.

This changed toward the end of the "Black" album and with *Live Shit: Binge & Purge*. Everyone sharing a bus became everyone having their own limo (not that I minded my own limo); with it also came bodyguards and the backstage became filled with people you didn't know telling you to "MOVE!", sometimes at least four feet. I, of course, took great umbrage at this; at one point Lars wanted to talk to me and made me wait outside his dressing room for five hours. I would do things like leave the show during the encores (as I had my own car) and Lars wouldn't even notice. It became no fun; me to them and them to me.

They came to me again after trying a couple of different photographers to shoot the *Load* tour. I had arrived early at a show in East Germany to find a day sheet (these are given to the band by the tour manager to let them know what's going on). On that day was written "Warning: Ross Halfin, be prepared; can be painful." Really nice to come back after a couple of years and see stuff like *that*. It was an okay shoot, but there was something lacking. I'd ask one of the bodyguards where they were and got a curt "don't know." Everything seemed to be "don't know." I shot my week of shows and took the money and thought, "Fuck it, they're paying, what does it matter?"

What mattered to me was that the camaraderie was gone. I'm sure they had a good time; I was just not part of it. My Metallica sabbatical lasted eleven years. I'd see them from time to time; I always stayed friendly with Kirk. Lars was a whole different story. We would run into each other occasionally in Los Angeles, as we stayed at the same hotel. Lars would always come over, shake my hand in the most insincere way, looking over my shoulder while he was doing it, to see who he could move on to in the room. We were sort of polar opposites. In 1999 I was doing an award show in London where I did portraits of the main artists. Four bodyguards came in, asked who I was, and told me that they were securing the room for Metallica. My son Oliver, who was ten at the time, was standing in the room; the bodyguard looked at him and said that "the fan has to leave." Oh, it was all friendly. . . . Eventually in came the band, who eyed me a bit warily, with Lars saying, "Don't do any pictures without the awards; he can sell them." Lars left as soon as he could and I had a chat with James, who was pleasant. I have to admit I felt very odd and quite alienated, considering how well I know them. I didn't see any of them again until 2004, when I saw Lars in a hotel lobby in Denmark. He made a point of coming over and introducing himself to my then girlfriend (who also happened to be Danish) and was charming. I was thinking "bollocks to him." My other half said, "Why can't you be nice?" She had a good point. He WAS nice and it was good to see him.

In 2007, Lars rang me and said, "Duder (yes, he really said Duder), how would you like to come out and shoot us?" I replied, "With which particular gun?" I started in Lisbon at the sound check. It was odd trying to figure out what they were going to do. By the second show I instinctively knew what they were going to do. Other photographers seem to be scared of them. The trick is to always take control of what you're doing and be able to read people. If I'm onstage looking close up at James I can tell when he doesn't want me up there. (This is being written halfway through the *Death Magnetic* tour and it is a pleasure being with them again.) Nowadays if I call or text Lars he replies. Metallica in older age are more thoughtful and prosaic. I asked Peter Mensch about Lars's phone call, he said, "Lars wanted me to call you, and I told him this is one phone call you are going to have to make." And, you know, I'm really pleased he did.

On the bus in the Midwest. I think we were on our way to the Iowa Jam, or Minneapolis. The weird thing was Metallica hadn't quite happened. They were the "in-between" band. Aerosmith, Ted Nugent, and Dokken were the main ones, and Metallica were sort of like "the fans playing to the fans." In these pictures, they *look* like fans, especially Lars and James, who really do look like punters; James could've been anyone in the audience. Which was what, in a weird way, gave them their charm.

– **R.H.**

I love this photo. Cliff Burton, backstage, Donington, 1985. And really, looking back at it now, this is the *ultimate* Cliff. It sums up who he was, how he was, and how he wanted to be perceived. He was always "up for it" because he understood what I wanted to do. Look at the shot with the denim jacket open and the Misfits shirt on the following page spread; Cliff got it. Even in the group shot opposite, he is the one member with the most confidence. The same can be said of the photo shoot at Butler's Wharf. By the way, Donington was a great show, but the audience hated them.

— **R.H.**

Classic 'Tallica. Look at all the debris on the stage. And I love the fact that you can see all this crap, this rubbish, everywhere. Remember, they were opening for Bon Jovi!

— **R.H.**

More Donington, this time from the front.
It was a pain in the arse shooting from the front because
you were just getting whacked by bottles of urine. Rather
them than me, obviously . . . I think in hindsight, to truly
understand the spirit of the gig, you had to have shot
from the stage. And this was one of the moments when
I realized that in order to get what I needed to get, I had
to be up there with them.

— **R.H.**

" . . . AJFA" tour, Hammersmith Odeon.
Shot from the mixing desk with a 180mm lens. "Justice is this, justice is that, justice is nine minutes long!" God, I used to hate that song, but truthfully, I don't mind it now. This shows Kirk, Jason, and Lars (with his sticks moving perfectly I might add) and James doing what they did best every night, with the full "Doris" production around them. I've been asked a lot over the years how to shoot a big production show. The thing is, it's not just about the show, it's about capturing the band delivering *with* the show and making sure that the excitement of all that gets caught without anything being missed. Also, you should really always shoot tours two weeks in, when everything is sorted out production-wise; but saying that, the band are always more likely to do stuff in the *first* two weeks because they're excited by the new production. Fine lines . . . you just have to use your experience to feel them out.

— **R.H.**

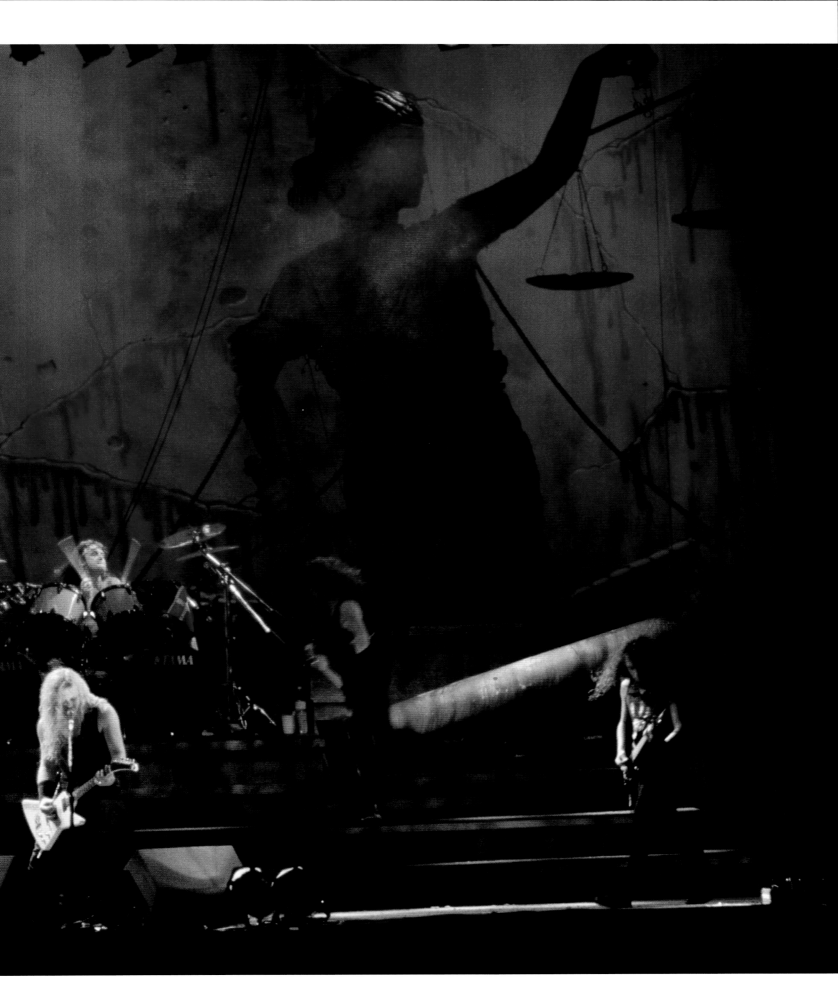

Bullet train in Japan, 1986. They were excited, it was new, it was fun, they were tourists. This is Tak (Udo, artist rep) with Lars. Looking at these now, the odd thing is that they wouldn't do pictures like this today, even though they are still tourists . . . sort of. On the right, it's the freezing snow halfway from Warsaw to Katowice (the Birmingham of Poland). It was Lars's idea to stop, of course. Look at the enthusiasm on James's face! Ironically, this is another thing they wouldn't do, because they rarely travel by road these days.

– R.H.

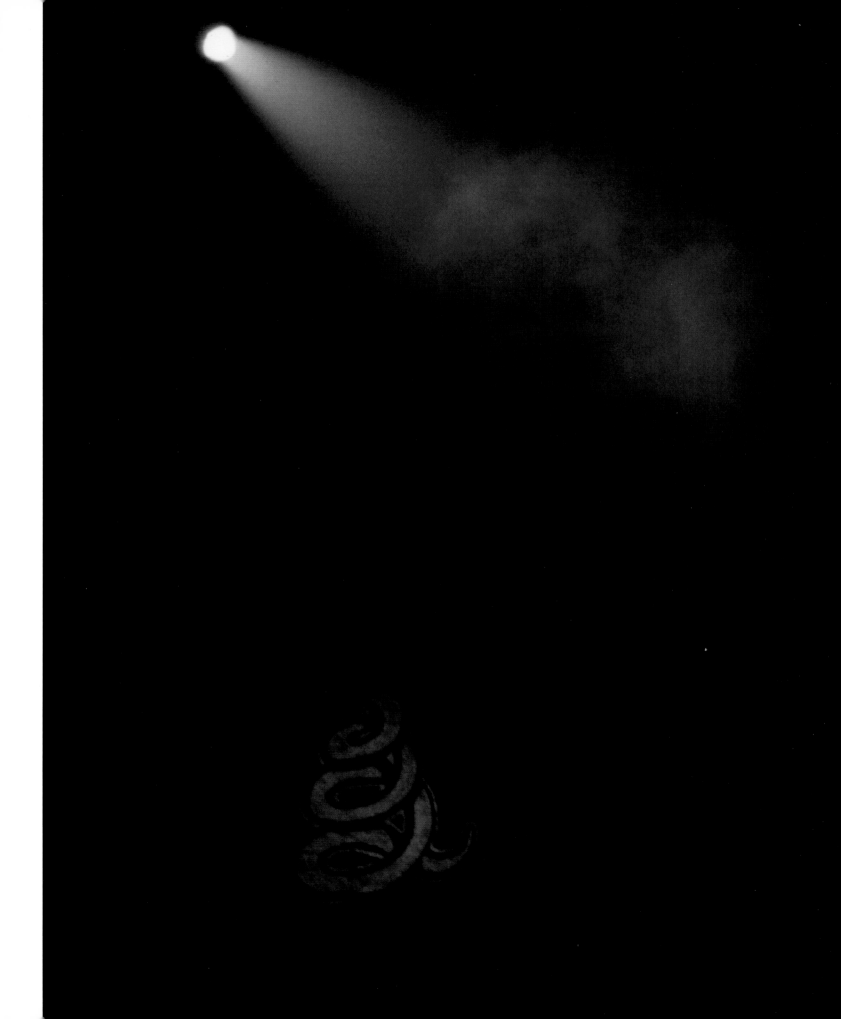

Monument Valley. The original idea was to shoot in the Badlands, which look like the moon. I went up there for the day a couple of days earlier, and it truly was fantastic, except it was very, very windy. Now remember, this was when Metallica had long hair, and it would've been blowing all over their faces, so I came up with the compromise of Monument Valley. It was quite a long shoot, and it didn't occur to me until I got there that God's light only lasts fifteen minutes . . . I like this picture. It definitely has something.

— **R.H.**

In One On One studios in LA recording the "Black" album. Everyone's always saying, "Wouldn't it be great to shoot a band recording in the studio." Let me tell you, kids, it is BORING. You can't move anything in or out, the band just wants to record, the engineer's paranoid that you'll touch something you shouldn't, you might also (gasp) learn a new song title you shouldn't know, and you're always in the way! Funnily enough, Bob Rock was happy to have his picture taken . . . then again, he's always been happy to have his picture taken!

– R.H.

Shoot done for promo for the "Black"
album. Hollywood. I'd flown to LA the week before and
done pictures and there was just no vibe. Lars said to go
home for a week, come back, and they'd get it together.
I did. And you know? So did they. One of my favorite
sessions with them. No assistants, no BlackBerrys, no
iPhones, no managers, no bodyguards. And you know
something? It can be most productive. Here's Lars "having
a moment . . ."

– R.H.

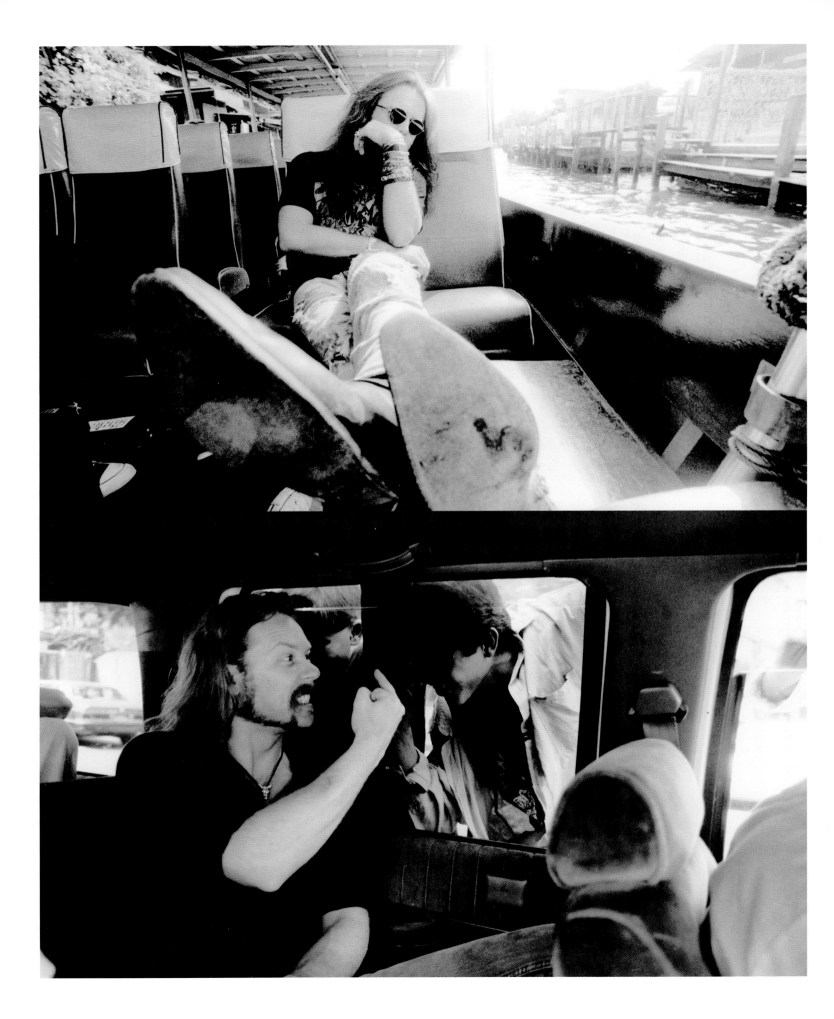

Kirk leading into ". . . Sanitarium."
With Kirk, he's always the most receptive to being shot, but always worried about how his hair looks . . . I mean Jesus, who cares? Always easy to shoot, always fun to shoot, and he has a great sense of humor, but then ALL of Metallica have a great sense of humor.

— **R.H.**

James backstage, Jakarta, Indonesia.
You'd never guess from this what was going on. It was an odd gig to start with, as the crew had split into two camps and seemed to be at war. It was a bit like *Mutiny on the Bounty*, and everybody was pissed off because of the long flights all over the place, from Australia to Southeast Asia. And then the kids set fire to the stadium! As we sat there watching the stadium burn, someone came up to us and said, "Don't you think you assholes should leave!!?" It was a fair question, and so we did. It was actually quite frightening, if I'm honest. I remember the extreme humidity and loads of people smashing on the windows of the bus as we tried to rush out, driving right through huge angry crowds.

— **R.H.**

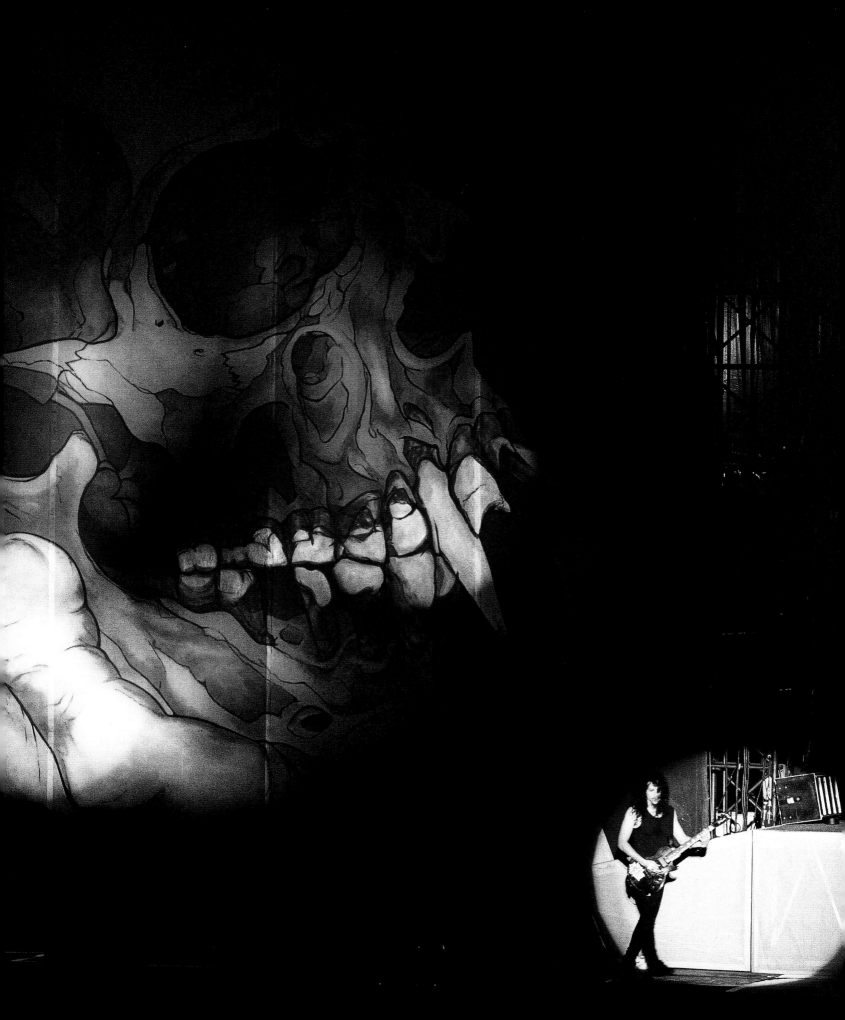

Los Angeles, a studio shoot right before the "Black" album came out. If you're going to shoot a band on a couch, this is the way to do it. I saw that couch and knew that you could take something that simple and turn it into something that was an immensely powerful image. It's really just all them in this photograph, as it should be. They look like a band not to be fucked with.

— **R.H.**

In the Valley, California. At the end of a long day shooting I was not into doing any more work. Lars was saying, "Let's shoot more and more," and looking back, I'm quite glad he pushed everyone to do it. The pool room itself was actually James's idea.

– R.H.

Lars in Tokyo with hidden hair. We were just wandering around Tokyo having a laugh. This was in the days now long gone when he would wake up (with a hangover) and WANT to do pictures. So we were walking along, and Lars saw some bloke's bike on the street, took it, and sat on it! Honestly, he would drive me mad to do pictures during this era, we're talking about . . . *Justice*. For example, I remember the first time they were in Sydney, Australia. I found a cave in a park that overlooks the opera house. Lars insisted on going down there three nights in a row, much to the chagrin of the rest of the band (James particularly)! At one point he wanted to do a time exposure like you do on a postcard; he wanted me to make the shot look like those postcard shots of Sydney at night. I pointed out to him that you need a tripod and a ten-minute exposure—that is, ten minutes of the band being completely still! He wouldn't believe me and happened to look around and see an old man taking night pictures of the opera house across the harbor. Guess who checked with the old man whether I was telling the truth?! Only Lars!!!

– R.H.

Tokyo. The second time they toured Japan. James sitting on the roof of a van in Shibuya. What you don't see is about a thousand people standing around watching us. This was before I had assistants, and I used to do it all on my own—lights, cameras, everything. It was just them, me, and a tour manager, and as soon as I'd finished shooting, the tour manager got into a van and very helpfully left. How nice! It was soon afterward that I realized I couldn't (and wouldn't) do it all alone and that I needed help. For me to focus on what I have to do, I need other people to focus on what I need set up.

– R.H.

ция
СТА

удии

"Ворот"

Н. Садур

ЧКА

(Гоголя «Вий»)

к С. Федотов

Телефон 33-66-12

оводитель театра
едотов

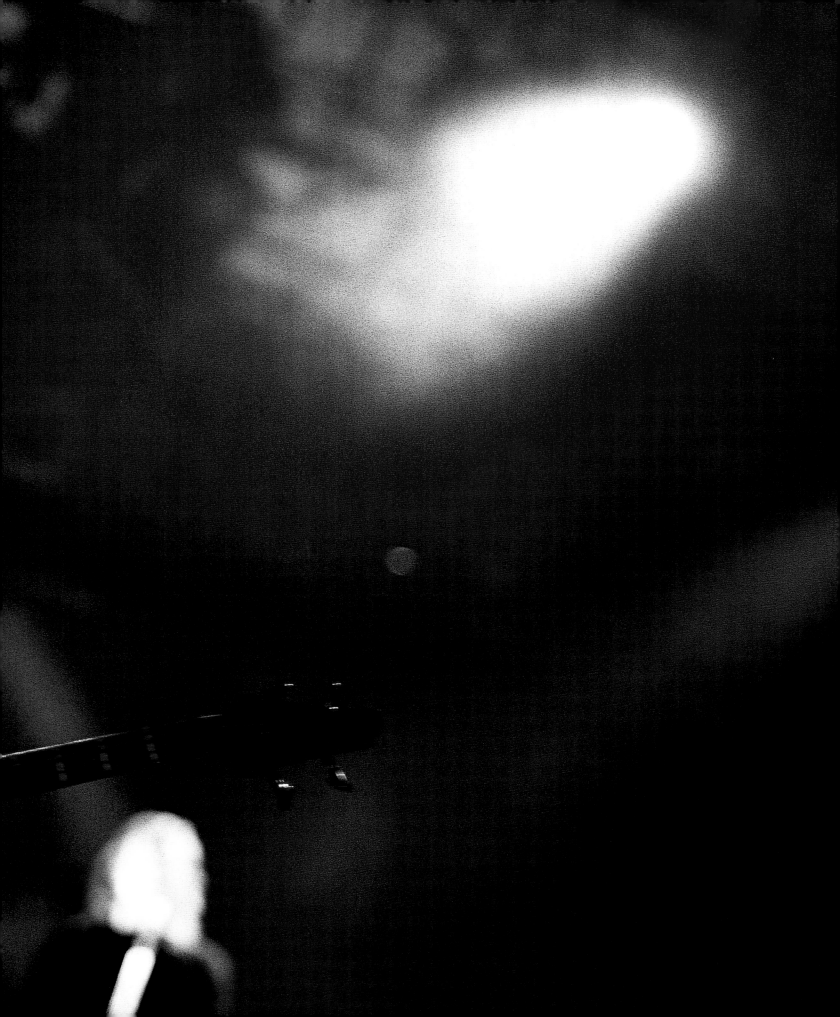

Spectrum, Oslo, Norway. The *Load* tour.
I didn't enjoy this at all. I had come back after a sabbatical,
and it was odd. Bodyguards, bodyguards, assistants, and
more bodyguards. I don't care what anyone says; there
was no vibe whatsoever, and everybody looks on edge.
I sensed there was no cohesion, and it seemed like they
were going in different directions.

– R.H.

Lars loved this picture at the time because I made him look like an Adonis. Taken at the Bercy in Paris. To shoot Lars live you have to get in there, and I don't mean just walk up there and stick a camera in his face—you won't get anything. You have to be able to read him, and much as he might not want to admit it, we both read each other very, very, very well.
— **R.H.**

Mexico City, Teotihuacán pyramids.
We were hounded by paparazzi on motorbikes with 1000mm lenses. I've never seen anything like it. James was determined not to pose for them. We ended up bribing the guard and shooting at 5 P.M. at the pyramids when no one was there. We ended up having a good time.

— **R.H.**

Phoenix, Arizona. First real production shoot of the *Death Magnetic* tour. I'd done Europe, but this was my first time in America with them on tour for a while. I fell into it quite easily . . . funny what you remember. I shot Albuquerque the next day; Lars wouldn't pick any of those because the stage was low, and it didn't have the whole production. These aren't shot with a massive Mamiya-like large-format camera; they're shot with a 35mm, and you simply have to get the balance right between the beams of light, the audience, and the client, i.e.: them. You also have to make sure that pit security in their bright yellow shirts don't show so much—yet another challenge. Something everyone should realize: it isn't as easy as point and shoot. I was up there for half the show making sure I got the shot.

– R.H.

Get in the van! Or the truck! Phoenix, Arizona, 2008. The drummer was convinced I was copying Anton (Corbijn). What he forgets is that I started way before his hero. I've always shot black-and-white from day one, which to put a date on it is 1975; Man playing at the Fairfield Halls in Croydon, and then AC/DC at the Marquee when they did a residency every Monday and Wednesday. I'll take AC/DC over Joy Division any day of the week.

– R.H.

Ah. The pyramids without paparazzi and
punters, at the end of the day. What more could you ask for?
— R.H.

Now, ladies and gentlemen, probably my favorite picture of the latest lineup era. I love both these pictures. The one on the left is taken in Werchter, Belgium, just as they'd come off stage, and the one on the right is just before their meet and greet in Tucson, Arizona. Can't remember what I did to make them laugh, but I like the fact the drummer didn't want to take pictures while he was smirking. I think this is true, natural, classic 'Tallica.

– R.H.

Mexico City. The original idea for the concert DVD was to have all crowd vibe shots and only a couple of the band. Of course this never happened. I quite like these pictures because the crowd in Mexico had so much energy. I will say that one of the most irritating things I go through is when people in the crowd are poking you while you're shooting and want to have some form of conversation. A conversation about what?!!!

– R.H.

Mexico City, Foro Sol, "Enter Sandman." What can I say? Me doing what I do. Great band. Great light show. Great pyro. Great crowd. Great show. The hard thing about pyro is you're not quite sure whether to overexpose it or underexpose it; it's very hit and miss. This is another time where I tend to rely on my instincts at the moment itself. This shot is taken from behind the band, the one three spreads later is taken from in front of them, and I like them both for obvious reasons.

– R.H.

(left) **James at the LA Forum, 2008. I wasn't** expecting him to jump, plus it was literally the last couple of frames I had left on the camera. Pleased I got it.

– R.H.

K. K. Downing eat your heart out!
"The Sinner"? No. It's THE RIPPER!

— R.H.

Nimes, France. Looked good; pain in the
arse to shoot. None of the security, who were all French and being typically "French," had any idea that I was going to be in there with a camera! I spent half the show fighting with them. The last show with the pyro going off at the top of the coliseum I only got because Rob Trujillo's wife, Chloé, being French, got me to the top just in time to get this. She fought valiantly, and successfully, for my cause.

– R.H.

ROSS AND METALLICA

YOU NEVER FORGET YOUR FIRST TIME
Paul Brannigan

My introduction to Metallica came via Ross Halfin's camera. It was the spring of 1986, and I was listening to the band's *Master of Puppets* album for the first time, but as the acoustic guitar intro to "Battery" spilled out of my stereo speakers I was barely paying attention, so engrossed was I in the photographs of the band on the album's inner sleeve. In the main picture, Cliff Burton, James Hetfield, Lars Ulrich, and Kirk Hammett are crammed together on their couch in the "Metallica Mansion," their shared house at 3132 Carlson Blvd., El Cerrito, California: beers aloft, fingers pointing into Halfin's lens, all bared teeth and cocksure, insouciant, "fuck you" attitude. The room is messy, with shit lying everywhere: God only knows what it smelled like. But with its Iron Maiden posters on the walls and crappy stereo in the corner, it didn't look that much different than my own teenage bedroom, and in their ripped jeans and faded T-shirts, Metallica didn't look very much different than my metalhead mates. To me, they looked like the coolest band in the world. Here, finally, was a band to believe in. Birth, School, Metallica, Death.

It was hard for a Metallica fan not to be jealous of Ross Halfin in the mid-'80s. In the pre-Internet age, when you couldn't hear Metallica on the radio, when the band had no videos, when they were still very much a word-of-mouth buzz, Halfin was our lifeline. He seemed to be always with the band—backstage, onstage, in the dressing rooms, on the tour buses, and weirdly, perhaps too often, in the shower. He was our eyes into their world, his photos the ultimate Access All Areas pass. I'd buy *Kerrang!* magazine every week for the smallest mention of Metallica: The writing was often terrible, always forgettable, but Halfin's photographs screamed with life and color, attitude and volume. In their earliest pictures, Metallica looks awkward and uncomfortable in front of the camera, but with Halfin orchestrating their shoots you can see that self-awareness melt away: In his *Master of Puppets*–era shots, you see only confidence and strength and self-belief; four young men united in the knowledge that this is their time.

Looking back from a time when every band's image is so carefully managed, manicured, and manipulated, there's an innocence and purity to these photos too. Halfin is never kept at arm's length, never held at a respectable distance from the band: He was a partner-in-crime, a catalyst for mischief and mayhem, but above all, he was family, and consequently his photos are unfiltered, raw and honest. Long before *Some Kind of Monster* drew back the curtain on the inner machinations of the Metallica machine, Halfin's photographs of the band are the real deal, reeking of sweat and alcohol and testosterone and adrenaline. Even when Metallica became the biggest rock band in the world with their phenomenal self-titled fifth album, his photos ensured that there was never a distance between the band and their fans, never any secrets, never any pretense. Metallica, you still felt, were one of us.

Somewhere along the line, as fame and ego and drugs clouded the picture, Ross Halfin and Metallica parted company. I'm not privy to the details, and I doubt either party can even remember what caused the schism.

Whatever. When Metallica returned in 2008 with *Death Magnetic,* an album that saw all their old fire, filth, and fury restored, it was surely no coincidence that Halfin was back in the frame, back in the pit, and back in the family—turning a mirror on the band once more, capturing images of four musicians who'd never looked more confident or more assured, their "hypnotizing power" at full blast. For old-school Metallica fans, and I'm proud to consider myself among that number, it felt right.

Paul Brannigan was the editor of Kerrang! *magazine from 2005 to 2009.*

A MAN OF MANY EXPLOITS
Phil Alexander

August, 1994. It's another nondescript Wednesday afternoon in London, where the British summer has once again taken a turn for the worse. In the confines of *Kerrang!*'s Carnaby Street HQ there's precious little going on as we contemplate the all-too-familiar prospect of finishing another issue of the world's only weekly metal magazine in the space of two days.

That is, until the office door crashes open and a small, gnarled, avuncular man stands before us. Dressed in his regulation black, faded shorts (designer, possibly blagged), white T (designer, definitely blagged), and a weighty leather man-bag (its bulge being attributable to a clutch of CDs, blagged, naturally), he begins his customary litany of scurrilous abuse. Targets include assorted musicians who've recently enjoyed the pleasure of his company ("He's the WRONG side of interesting!") and hapless publicists ("He was too busy GROVELING to sort out the shoot!"). Ross Halfin has returned from yet another expedition and is regaling us with his "joyous" exploits.

This time around, as well as shooting a plethora of other acts, Ross has spent time on the road with his "CPFs" (that's "Close Personal Friends" in Halfin-speak) in Metallica. The fruits of his trek consist of a ton of pictures —and by a ton, I mean a veritable avalanche of 35mm transparencies. The first sheet of forty posed pictures, he declares, includes "the cover shot for the next issue." There are also at least thirty sheets of live shots where Ross appears to have documented every single facial expression pulled by Metallica during their fifty-date "Shit Hits the Sheds" tour. Then, come another twenty-odd sheets of backstage shots capturing the unsuspecting band members in various states of repose and relaxation. . . .

There's a post-show Lars Ulrich looking contemplative, sitting alone in his dressing room ("Look, it's Stars!"); there's James Hetfield holding a pair of fake devil horns to his forehead and gurning with mock menace ("How very metal of him!"); Jason Newsted meanwhile is grimacing in the back of the band's tour bus ("Typically, Newkid was busy moaning!"); oh, and there's Kirk Hammett, sporting his new dreadlocks and pierced lip, and, er, standing naked in a dressing room with a pink shower cap on his head.

"You should use that as the center-spread next issue! He'll love it!" enthuses Halfin.

And so, we do. . . .

The issue of *Kerrang!* cover dated August 20, 1994, boasts a shot of all four Metalli-chaps with the additional alluring cover line of "Kirk Hammett Starkers Stunner." Inside, the poster caption of said "Stunner" reads "One for the Ladies."

Subsequently we find out that Kirk doesn't "love it" after all.

Strangely, Ross, however, does.

And somehow, this story perfectly sums up Ross Halfin's relationship with Metallica over the years.

James Hetfield once described the pleasure of working with Ross as being "as much fun as shaving your head with a cheese grater while chewing on a cactus." He was not entirely wrong. Having said that, no one has truly managed to capture the very essence of what Metallica is all about in the manner that Ross has.

There is a larger-than-life quality to Halfin's work with the band that matches their sound and attitude. His live shots—secured by rampaging across the band's stage with a callous disregard for their own personal space—are truly epic. His backstage material, as Kirk will no doubt attest, is truly revelatory and crushingly candid. ("It's called REPORTAGE!" he bellows, while never quite being able to spell the word.) And his session work is iconic, amplifying both the band's sense of mischief and their magnitude.

Metallica have worked with Ross since 1984. I have worked with him since 1991. These days we still work together when he contributes to *MOJO*. So I've known him long enough to safely state that for all his bullish exterior, Ross also has a more sensitive (and, admittedly, rarely seen) side, yet in his work he has never forgotten why he is there: to get the job done. This book clearly illustrates that very fact. Rather touchingly, it also reinforces the fact that Metallica and Ross deserve each other. And, deep down, they know it too. . . .

Phil Alexander is the editor-in-chief of MOJO *and* Kerrang! *magazines.*

THANK YOU, ROSS . . .
Paul Rees

. . . and I say that because the truth is I have
Ross Halfin to thank for getting me into Metallica, and vice versa (although the latter experience has brought along with it the more dubious pleasures). Before their unholy union with Ross came about, Metallica seemed to me nothing but pimply oiks who sang, daftly, about putting "metal up your ass." To someone reared on Sabbath, Motörhead, and AC/DC—properly big beasts of the rock jungle—Metallica were, well, silly.

My first exposure to them came through the pages of *Kerrang!* magazine. So, too, did I then become aware of the name Ross Halfin, since it usually appeared alongside photographs of hairy, gurning men (always men), who for some reason had been crammed into a shower or urinal and stripped to their underwear (and in those days Y-fronts or, worse, leather codpieces were very much en vogue). It perhaps goes without saying that these were grubby, unedifying spectacles, and so too I dismissed Ross, in his case as the peddler of some strange form of homoerotic heavy metal soft porn.

I was, though, as ignorant of the man-with-the-camera's background at *Sounds* magazine (making punk 'erberts and metal upstarts alike appear impossibly exciting) as I was of the flowering of Metallica into a band every bit as monumental as the aforementioned triumvirate. Happily, for me at least, the two then began working together.

It's pointless here going over the degree to which Halfin not only captured the spirit of Metallica but also elevated them to an iconic level, because the pictures herein tell that story for themselves. But it should be noted that they're among the grandest, most honest, and thrilling portfolio any rock band has been privileged enough to lay claim to.

One shot, though, will always spring to my mind: It's the "Black" album tour, James Hetfield is onstage at some vast open-air gig; he's shot from below, in black and white, stalking the borders of the snakepit, arms outstretched to the masses. He is gigantic, heroic . . . it is an indelible image of rock's primal power.

In retrospect it's no wonder the two parties clicked. Both were entirely free of bullshit and compromise; both balls of fire and fury. Neither would be considered hip, cool, or any of those other dreadful words by the then cognoscenti, and neither would have cared. There were, too, striking similarities between drummer and photographer, physically and in the sense that neither would ever shut the fuck up.

They parted ways, of course. I have some empathy with Metallica here—Ross could test the patience of a whole army of saints. But they weren't the same without him. . . .

It may be coincidence that Ross's return to the job of documenting Metallica came at the same time as their best album in years, *Death Magnetic*.

But I don't think so. They were made for each other.

Paul Rees is the editor-in-chief of Q *magazine.*

EYE OF THE BEHOLDER
Brad Tolinski

Photographers are the great unsung heroes of rock 'n' roll. When we think of music's biggest stars, it is often through the photographer's remarkable lens. If you find that an overstatement, close your eyes for a moment and summon up the image of your favorite band or musician.

If you love the early Beatles, your mind's eye probably sees some variation on Dezo Hoffman's brilliant, icon-making early '60s photos of the boys leaping in the park, or perhaps Robert Freeman's moody shots of the Fab Four on the cover of *With the Beatles*.

How about the Doors? No matter how bloated and bearded singer Jim Morrison got toward the end of his short life, he'll always be the bare-chested young lion captured by Joel Brodsky in his remarkable 1967 photo shoot. And would U2 have the same gravitas without Anton Corbijn's black-and-white portraits of the band etched in our brains? It's doubtful.

The greatest rock artists have always had at least one photographer capable of capturing the essence of who they are, a fellow traveler and artist who can produce an image that makes the rest of the world sit up and take notice . . . and understand.

It's not clear that Metallica would have become the same commercial juggernaut without the brilliant photos of Ross Halfin. One thing is for certain: Halfin's polished images of them elevated the group above the heavy metal rabble and helped pave the way for Metallica's crossover success in the eighties and nineties.

It's hard to remember, but back in 1983 Metallica were just another spotty underground metal band in black jeans and T-shirts. Among a small circle of hard-rock aficionados they were considered the best of a growing subgenre of metal called "thrash." But to the casual rock fan there was little to distinguish them from any of the other scruffy longhaired boys playing this hard, fast, and unapologetically brutal new music.

Even after thrash began gaining some momentum, bands like Slayer, Anthrax, Megadeth, Exodus, and Testament were roundly ignored by the mainstream, because, unlike punk, the rock cognoscenti never considered metal "cool."

But, somehow, Metallica were a little different.

When pictures of the band—*Ross Halfin's pictures of the band*—began to make their way into the media, Metallica stood out. Their photos were clearly hipper and more interesting than the usual corny, poorly lit studio shots of other metal groups. Ross's unique fish-eye-lens images and arty black-and-white pictures revealed a group that was at times cocky, funny, commanding, ironic, dangerous, and even (*gasp!*) handsome. You could see their humor and intelligence, and the photos made you want to be part of their world, regardless of your musical preference.

Not that any of this was contrived. The members of Metallica had all of these qualities, but it took Halfin's well-lit, ingeniously composed images to vividly bring out the best in them. He made Metallica appear both larger-than-life *and* completely accessible. But perhaps his greatest service to the band was with his phenomenal live shots, which captured the energy of Metallica's preposterously exciting concerts.

Halfin's first encounter with the band took place in 1984. It was less than auspicious. Q Prime, a rock 'n' roll management team, had previously hired him to shoot Def Leppard, one of its biggest acts. Pleased with his work, Q Prime dispatched the British photographer to San Francisco to shoot some publicity stills of its latest signing, Metallica. At the time, the group was preparing to release *Ride the Lightning*, its second full-length effort. Ross was unfamiliar with Metallica, and the only instruction he received from Q Prime was to "see if you can talk the bass player out of wearing flares," a reference to bassist Cliff Burton's hopelessly retro bell-bottom jeans.

Halfin arrived on the West Coast expecting to meet The Next Big Thing. Instead, he was greeted by four scrawny, half-starving musicians living communally in a house with a pathetically empty refrigerator. His first idea was to go out and buy some food, set up a feast, and photograph the boys whooping it up à la the Rolling Stones' classic *Beggar's Banquet* album cover. Unfortunately, by the time Ross got set up, the band had consumed all the food. Halfin failed to persuade bassist Burton to ditch his flared denim trousers, but he did get the band members to relax and let down their guard. Metallica saw a bit of themselves in Halfin's caustic sense of humor and take-no-prisoners attitude, and in time he became like part of the group. Eventually they stopped posing for the camera and began simply responding to the belligerent, and often hilarious, person behind the camera. If Metallica look like they are having a riot in their pictures, it's often because they are.

The long-running joke between the group and the photographer is his general disdain for their music. While it's true Ross was not particularly crazy about Metallica's break-neck rhythms and relentless guitars, he did like the band members, and their relationship became one of the great symbiotic creative unions in the history of modern music, lasting well over a decade.

Hetfield, in particular, flourished in front of Halfin's lens. View photos of the singer/guitarist chronologically and you can see him evolve from a gangly mutt to one of metal's great commanding presences. Like a superhero belted by gamma rays, James morphs into the great, implacable, always cool Fonz of Metal. And thus it remained.

Until it ended.

In the second half of the nineties, the group stopped using Halfin and began to favor trendy photographers. It's no coincidence that many pictures of Metallica from that era ring false and look dated. Hetfield appears moody and deflated, and his band mates look decadent and foppish, lacking the danger they once so casually wielded.

Photography can be about technique, but technique alone yields the forgettable. More often, a compelling shot is about the relationship between the photographer and the subject. Without that connection, no amount of darkroom razzmatazz or digital trickery will make a strong image.

Ross Halfin certainly possesses technique. Like a great athlete, he has a sharp eye, incredible reflexes, amazing instinct, and the gift of anticipation. But he has other gifts as well. He makes people laugh. He makes them angry. He puffs them up and then punctures them when he needs them to be human. His quick wit and imagination take even the biggest stars by surprise, and when people are surprised, they act natural. It is at that moment he goes in for the kill and captures his prey.

Ross has always understood that there is something inherently badass about Metallica. They don't have to act that way—they just are. The only time they cease to be badass is when they try. When they work with other photographers, you can often see the effort. When they work with Ross, their true colors shine naturally, because Ross can smell bullshit a mile away, and he won't let them even go there.

In recent years, Ross and the band have resumed their working relationship. Ross still doesn't like their music much, and there are times when the band doesn't like Ross much. But as in the good old days, they keep each other real, and they still make great pictures.

Don't think Ross Halfin is a huge part of Metallica and their music? Go ahead: Close your eyes and think of the band, and I'll bet you see one of the fantastic images in this book.

Brad Tolinski is the editor-in-chief of Guitar World *and* Guitar Aficionado *magazine.*

WE'RE A HAPPY FAMILY
Steffan Chirazi

***Unique* is a word that gets abused on a daily** basis, as in "oh, they're *so* unique!" when they're usually about as unique as a traffic light.

So trust me when I tell you that Ross Halfin is unique.

And trust me further when I say that his relationship with Metallica, his familial relationship with Metallica, is about as close as you can get to blood ties without a single common gene.

They say you choose your friends but are born with family. Ha ha ha, if ever there was a man to undo clichés, it is—yes, you guessed it—Ross. Because, yes, Metallica chose to seek Halfin's professional expertise back in the day, fired up by the man's bombastic heavy-metal reputation, his work with the Maidens and Motörheads of this world, and his globetrotting on behalf of

Sounds magazine. But that's where the "choose friends" bit ends and the "born with family" bit gets twisted around. Yes, they chose Ross, but this relationship took on a lively familial flavor pretty much from the get-go.

When entering the work arena, Halfin has always struck first, his deft, bludgeonesque combination of sarcasm and volume quickly leveling the playing field and sorting out the chancers from the lifers. PRs, corporates, bullshitters, and occasionally even oneself were often referred in a cacophonous roar of indignant "FUCK OFFS" and "TIME-WASTING, ARSE-KISSING WANKERS." To a young band of "fuck-you" kids like Metallica, it was a fire-and-gasoline combination that saw great results: Halfin would use his experience and reputation to cajole (yell at) them into shots no one else could get, and Metallica were happy to return abusive fire at the lensman whenever said shots were taken. Nobody dozed off bored when the two got together.

And as is Halfin's way, their stage was his stage because (put simply) how else are you going to get a half-decent live photo unless you get in there and make the thing happen? Wait for an invitation, and you'd die of frostbite; Ross, as you might've noticed, has always had a deep tan.

Halfin and the band were like a teenage gang fighting the world, and sometimes like teenage siblings pissing each other off. Love-ins and love-outs. The name of familial games the world over. But one thing that never wavered was the work. Halfin would shove his lens wherever it needed to go, and Metallica would let that lens be shoved. Which is why his live shots of the band remain unparalleled.

In the mid-'90s, the balance of this familial relationship turned sour. Who knows the specifics? Probably buried in the fact that these were, er, unique characters, none of whom were willing to cede an inch of turf over something that was probably no more than familiarity breeding contempt. They needed a cooling-off period, and they took one. A long one. And then, one day, Halfin was back on tour. Just like that. I'm not even sure they actively discussed the decade that had passed, the avoidance of such a discussion in itself a curiously familial act.

It's much nicer these days. Halfin has certainly calmed down, and although he still doesn't suffer fools gladly or otherwise, he no longer approaches the world waving a broadsword. And Metallica too have mellowed, being more communicative, more discussive, and generally easier to work with.

Anyone can take a photo of a band, and many ones have shot Metallica around the world. But as you already know, Halfin captures them internationally in a way that no one else has ever emulated. Because he knows them. And they know him. And because family, however much they might fight, remains instinctual and inseparable family.

Steffan Chirazi is the editor of So What! *magazine.*

ROSS HALFIN: A conversation with Steffan Chirazi

Steffan Chirazi: Could you offer your first recollections of meeting Metallica?

Ross Halfin: I thought they were children. You've got to understand that I'd been shooting for quite a while. And you know, I don't mean this in an arrogant way, Lars seemed to know more about what I did than I did. I think the one thing that impressed them was that they had a poster of Michael Schenker on the wall when he was in his band MSG [Michael Schenker Group] and I'd taken that picture. I remember thinking that James was very quiet, Lars was very . . . what's the right word? . . . very knowledgeable and enthusiastic. Kirk was just the way Kirk is really, mellow, easygoing, and Cliff looked at me with a sort of distant contempt, the irony of which is that I got on with him really well later on. You know, I was told by Peter Mensch (one of Metallica's managers, alongside Cliff Burnstein) that my main job was to get him to take his flares off. I remember that we shot outside, but it was really like shooting a bunch of kids. It really wasn't like shooting an established band, but then again, that was their charm. I think Metallica appealed to the kids because they were *like* the kids.

SC: But there must have been something in them that appealed to you as well.

RH: Oh yes, there was always a very good sense of humor, which is hard for an American band; well, considering one of them's Danish! But they always had a very good sense of humor, which I feel I sort of helped them learn as well, you know, the ability to see the funny side of things in most situations. Another thing I remember is that they were sort of hugely annoying in their own annoying way. I remember doing an early picture with food, and they were so hungry because they had no money, they ate all the food! Which meant I had to buy some more. I ended up buying their groceries the first time I met them, which is quite funny looking back but was quite aggravating at the time. Looking back on those pictures in that house, it was like being in a fifteen-year-old kid's bedroom.

SC: So you were what, twenty-seven, twenty-eight? So you were still just about at an age where you could identify with their teenage-like goofiness?

RH: Yes, but I did have some form of authority.

SC: What was the first moment you remember getting them in step with what this sort of photography needed?

RH: Well, that first time was very hard because they were just like fans. And then I think we went on the road to the Iowa Jam. . . . Oh, I can tell you the first time I thought they looked really good was when I shot them in the snow, in Denmark, when they were making *Master of Puppets* at Sweet Silence studios in Denmark; would've been late '84, I think. I thought they actually started to look like Metallica then, as you'd want Metallica to look. Because before that they were always a bit, you know, "fans in a band" looking. Someone was in an Iron Maiden T-shirt, someone was in skintight jeans, someone was doing this. But this time they were actually starting to get their "look" with the leathers and whatnot. . . .

SC: You shot them in the road as well, that misty road, during the same time? I think it was one of the promo shots. I remember it ran with a feature I did in *Sounds* on the band.

RH: Well, there was a misty road, but that was the Golden Gate Bridge. And the idea was to shoot them at the Golden Gate Bridge at dusk. Except the fog rolled in, and it didn't really work.

SC: When they were crouching down?

RH: Yeah, yeah, yeah. That's absolutely above the Golden Gate Bridge. It was absolutely freezing, and Cliff drove us in his truck.

SC: Let's talk about their humor. Do you think the fact they were softened up by a Birmingham road crew helped your communication process, and as a result your work with them? After all, you have a strong sense of sarcasm yourself, which can disarm people if they're not prepared for it.

RH: Well, they were Anglophiles. They knew all the English bands. They were fans of the English bands. They liked Thin Lizzy, who were of course fronted by an Irishman, but you get what I'm saying, Black Sabbath, and UFO. Three bands that I did, that I shot, and I worked with Iron Maiden, whom they loved. You know, I wasn't the first-choice photographer to shoot Metallica. Originally they'd shot with Fin Costello because he did Deep Purple. But they just looked, you know, plainly stupid. And I was brought in by Mensch to "make a band" out of them, if you like.

SC: And let's talk about their energy, of them as a live act that first time you shot them onstage.

RH: Well . . . the first time I shot them live was at the Lyceum, London in 1984 on *Ride the Lightning*. And I thought they were so amateurish it was quite endearing and fun. But for me, that was their charm back then, the fact that they were unpolished, which of course they now aren't. I remember the first time I really realized they were a serious force as a band, let alone a live band, and that was at a show at the Palladium in LA, when they opened for Armored Saint with Adam Bomb in 1985. And it's the only show

I've ever seen where the support act devastated the headliner . . . and they really did.

SC: So if it hadn't have been for Mensch forcing the union, or whatever you want to call it, do you think you'd have chosen to shoot them again after those first few times.

RH: No. I don't think I would have followed it up. I've got to give Mensch his due. He understood how we'd get on and work well together, and we [Ross and Metallica] actually forged a good relationship. I started to enjoy working with them.

SC: Do you think that Mensch understood the personalities? Because you and Lars share a very, very sharp sense of sarcastic humor.

RH: Yeah, but I taught Lars to be sarcastic!

SC: Which is frightening.

RH: I only know this because they were watching football once and Dave Brock, who's their U.K. travel agent, went in the room. This was, by the way, years later, during our working "hiatus" in the '90s. And Lars apparently said to Dave, "It's just about twenty-two men kicking a piece of leather." Dave asked him where he got that from, and Lars went, "Ross Halfin."

SC: But the pair of you do share a deep, deep passion for music, too. I think people who just read your blog might not actually realize that you like music as much as you do. You love The Who and Led Zeppelin, for example.

RH: I like music in the same way Lars likes music, yes. Lars likes listening to Tank or Diamond Head in the same way I like listening to The Who and Zeppelin. We're fans ourselves.

SC: Did you feel you had to "own" the band in order to "break" them into doing what you wanted?

RH: I don't know if it's exactly like that. My thing, jokingly, was always to treat them like they were at school and I was in charge. And it did have a benefit for a long time, because I tried to bring their personality out of them and make them laugh. And I like to think that the first ten years, even though they may look at it now and think it's a bit twee or embarrassing or whatever, that is the look of Metallica that people know. And it is the look of Metallica that people want. You know, someone like Anton Corbijn can shoot them, but that's not Metallica. So he can do these album covers but it's not Metallica because it's a stylized look that's, you know, it could be U2. It could be REM. It could be Depeche Mode. It could be anyone else he shoots. And I like to think that how I shot them gives them the look that is Metallica. You know, I can make them look tough, I can make them look threatening but I also make them look fun.

SC: When does a photographer feel like it's *his* band?

RH: Well, I'm purely recognized for two bands, really. Iron Maiden and Metallica. Really I am. And the other thing is, I can communicate with people when I want to, and they can communicate back. Metallica can be difficult and painful, but when they want to do something, I'll give them their due, they do it. And they go out of their way to do it properly. They really do. Lars and James particularly know what kids want. Plus you, as a photographer, should always take charge of what you do. Because if you don't take charge of what you do, and you don't make it your platform, then it's not your picture.

SC: When did you learn that?

RH: I shot Robert Plant when I first started, and I was like, "Wow, it's Robert Plant." I walked up to him and he was a total—he was appalling to deal with! He leaned into me and he said, "Do you know how to take a Robert Plant picture?" And I went, "No, how?" And he went, "Quickly." And he said it nastily. And I didn't take a good picture because I took a picture that Robert Plant wanted to take. And after that day I vowed that no one would intimidate me at a photo shoot, and I've always stuck by that. If someone wants to do that, I will leave. Again, you've got to do what you want it to be, because otherwise it's not your photo. It's someone else's. I have walked away from people who were just being impossible.

SC: Do time constraints on a photo shoot become irritating?

RH: If everything is clear up front time-wise, then no. I can make something that's shot in ten minutes look like I was there an hour. And I don't think I'm difficult to deal with. If you tell me I have ten minutes to do a shoot, I can accept that. If you tell me I have five minutes, I can accept that as long as I know up front. If you tell me I've got two hours, I can accept that. But I will be difficult if you tell me I've got an hour and it turns into four minutes.

SC: Which appears to be a hallmark of how things work.

RH: If you let them work that way. And this is why when people say, "Oh, it's all right for *you*," I mean, it's not all right for me! I actually like to think I work quite hard. And I also think that part of working quite hard is knowing when, and how, to stand your ground in given situations. It's also one of those things bands, management, and people can't take: that is the word "no." And then when they sit and go "you have to," you stand your ground and say no. I started realizing that in the late '70s and early '80s with American bands, they'd say, "You can do this blah blah blah, you have to stop doing this blah blah blah," and I'd just say no, which would leave them very aggravated and confused. But it was very simple for me; I'm here to do my job, let me do it properly.

SC: When did you first truly learn the power of the word "no" in a working situation?

RH: It was Dogs D'Amour in LA. They thought they were the next big thing. They made some stupid demands, so I walked out of it. I once did

Smashing Pumpkins, same thing. I'll give you a prime example of when the rules got so many I walked out, and that was shooting Pearl Jam. I mean seriously, for the people's band, they've got more rules than the Army.

SC: Looking back through the eras with Metallica, early on there's the image of this young bunch of scruffs who are shooting upwards. How did you manage to tame that energy enough to produce the images you all wanted to see?

RH: Well, I was very firm with them. There was some stuff where we were messing around, in Japan and stuff, but generally I wouldn't let them mess around. They might've joked around a bit, and that was important because you do have to have fun, but all the silly pictures like Alcoholica [from a 1984 session by a different photographer in which the Metallica logo was altered to read "Alcoholica"], and you know, burning drumsticks, and stuff like that, I would never tolerate any of that. That "metal pie" and Lars sprayed silver was a big one for me because I actually didn't like it! The idea is always to make a band look like you want to be in that band, or at the very least that you think they look good. I didn't do a studio session for a long, long time. When they did a studio session for *Ride the Lightning* with Fin Costello they hated it, particularly Cliff, and so they vowed never to do a studio shoot. And then I got them to do one with Jason when he first joined the band. It was in London at Holborn Studios. They still fought. They still wouldn't do it properly. They were uncomfortable doing it. They thought it was crap because they thought it was posing. I suppose I can take credit for talking them into doing it. They would laugh about shooting against "the white wall." James would sarcastically go, "Wow, we've flown all over the world for another white wall." He's being sarcastic. But I made sure they knew that's all you need, because it's the band that projects, not the location or the backdrop.

SC: Let's talk about Cliff for a moment. It seems to me that what you're suggesting with Cliff is that perhaps having been the frostiest on entry, you ended up having a deep respect for each other.

RH: Yes, that's true, we did have a deep respect for each other. Cliff also carried a lot of weight in the band. He respected what I did and I respected what he did in a joking sort of way. I remember I shot them during the Cliff era in Chicago, in a stairwell. . . . I also shot them in a setup in Butler's Wharf, which is the south side of Tower Bridge [in London] and which was all run-down at the time. And I think that was one of the defining images in terms of when they first looked really good. I succeeded in getting them to properly stop messing around and be serious.

SC: You told me once that Peter Mensch asked you to get Cliff to stop wearing flared trousers.

RH: Oh, I did. I said, I didn't say Peter Mensch, but I said to Cliff, "Why don't you change your trousers?" And he's like, "No way." And I think truthfully, Lars wanted me to try and get him to take them off. But I was onto a loser there, because Cliff did what he wanted. And that's why I had a very great respect for him at the time. He did it his way.

SC: Let's revisit some of the early locations, some early adventurous moments.

RH: Early on, we didn't really have the money to go and do anything. Everything was always done on a tight budget, so we'd just stop the bus and go and do something somewhere. Wherever looked good. I'd say, "Why don't we do some pictures here?" and we'd stop the bus and pile out. I remember after Cliff died we ended up in Alaska on the way back from Japan, and I suggested shooting on a glacier. So Lars goes and hires a helicopter! You know, I've got to give it to them. They were right there. And when they said, "Yeah, let's get a helicopter!" it typified the spirit of the time. We then flew up on this glacier that was really, really dangerous because it was like skating on something you couldn't control. And it was freezing. And we spent the whole afternoon shooting up there.

SC: It's probably the case that when a band is younger, with perhaps less personal obligations, they will go the extra mile to do things like long photo sessions on location.

RH: Yes, sure. We'd go to Australia and we'd go out! We'd roam round looking for things. I remember being in Germany on the "Black" album, they had three days off so I convinced them to go to Faro to see Steve Harris's Harry's Bar. But really, we went there to do pictures. And I've gotta give it to them, they did pictures for four or five hours.

SC: So the glacier shoot was memorable . . .

RH: Yeah. There have been other ideas, and some other great locations of course. I originally wanted to shoot them in the Badlands because it looks like the moon out there, but we ended up not going there because it was so windy and they had long hair! So we ended up going to Monument Valley just purely because it was dry with no wind. I particularly like that shot of them at the LA Coliseum from the *Monsters of Rock* tour in 1988; I shot them halfway up those big steps leading onto the stage with the whole audience and the stage behind them. And I think that's a really good shot because they're really enjoying themselves. They look relaxed, but they also look like a great band.

SC: Festival gigs are always a good time.

RH: Yes. I remember their first Donington in 1985 when Bon Jovi headlined I think; I shot them just hanging out backstage in their trailer. Where they had nothing. They went onstage and everybody was throwing stuff at them! There's mud and everything around the stage. But you know, they won, though. And that is a sign of a great band and a great moment. Just at the time I'm thinking, "Oh, no, all this stuff's flying, they're fucked, the photos are fucked, it's not good." And looking at the pictures now they're actually really good. I think they're very strong.

SC: Do you find it enjoyable shooting them live?

RH: I do enjoy it. It's not always easy . . . shooting the "Black" album when it was in the round was hard work. The stage was high, it was at awkward angles, and you had to shoot it from certain bits of the setup. I mean, of course I got to know the show and in doing so, I got to know how to get what I wanted from it. But that was very hard work.

SC: I'm sure you probably spend a show or two just taking notes on every tour you go out on, right? Just so as you can get a strong picture of where certain moments are most likely to occur.

RH: Yes, you do. Usually the first three shows, waiting for them to get the light show right, and just making sure everything is set.

SC: I think it's your live work which has catapulted you into a sphere of your own.

RH: Well I like to think that one of the things I specialize in is capturing the moment between them and a crowd, which I feel I'm always good at getting. All those shots of them lining up onstage and turning round to face me, the ones with the crowd behind them, was always my idea. Which everyone has sort of stolen now. But that shot is always so powerful because it's a purely distilled moment of the audience and them all becoming one.

SC: Do you think that the length of the relationship has allowed you to personally, and physically, get closer to them, especially onstage?

RH: You know, I'm sure it has, and they trust my eye. But I also know *how* to shoot them live. Everybody thinks you just stick a lens in front of James, go "bang, bang, bang," and you'll get something. You don't. The moment to capture James is when he slightly leaves the mike for a second. And that is a hard thing to get, but I know how to get it. Even though I kid around about it, I actually *do know* their music, I know how they work live and I know how they move live.

SC: I think it's fair to say that in terms of live photography you certainly pushed the parameters for everyone, because you made it completely acceptable for a photographer to walk onto the stage and stand three feet from the musician. Which is a tough thing to do both physically and mentally. It'd be very easy to feel like your were intruding.

RH: Yes, okay, I hear what you're saying, but what people don't get with that is that I'm good at reading them. Just from doing it a long time, and you've *got* to be able to read someone's body language and know when it's an okay time to do it and when it's not an okay time to do it. You don't just walk up and go "bang, bang, bang, bang, bang"; you have to communicate with that person and read that person. It sounds a bit weird, but you have to be able to almost telepathically read them, read their body, read what they're doing, and what they do and don't want you to do. When I go and shoot, say, James or Lars onstage, I know when it's good or not good to do certain things.

SC: I think one of the things that people perhaps don't appreciate is you don't have to talk to people all the time in order to be close.

RH: No, I think they just have to know you. And however anyone else might shoot them, and this is not me being arrogant or bigheaded, the thing is that I understand them, I understand what they do, when they do it, and how they do it. And I also understand what they want to project.

SC: And let's talk about trust for a moment. Because I think that beneath everything in this relationship with them, beneath the back and forth, the complaints, the praise, the rows, beneath all of it, there has developed an enormously deep sense of trust. They know if they ask you to do something, they're going to get it. And likewise, it appears to me that you know you're going to get every tool you need to get the job done. So trust must be an enormous part of this relationship, right?

RH: Oh absolutely, yes. I think I know when to leave them alone. Is that the right way to put it? I know when they want to do something and when they don't. And you'll find that you always get more out of them if, you know . . . it's hard to explain . . . it's sort of . . . I know "the moment." I think that's the best way to put it.

SC: In a way taking a tenuous tangent from that, when you look back at that, do you think all your time spent on the marathon "Black" album tour

RH: Yes. Absolutely. I think they just got absolutely exhausted out there . . . there were lots of things, really. Also, I think Lars just really wanted to work with Anton [Corbijn]. And I think after the decade's breather, they found a new appreciation for what I do and how we work, and brought me back. And you know, we've got on well again since. I have to admit, I was really devastated when they replaced me. I must admit that.

SC: Interesting. Because I think the initial reactions were more of defiance?

RH: Well, I was really, really shocked. And more by the fact that Lars never told me. I just didn't hear anything and then they had someone else. It wasn't as much that I held a grudge, I just felt I'd lost a friend in Lars at that time. And I like to think now that we have totally rekindled that. You know, he's still infuriating in his own way. But now, if you ask Lars to ring you, he will ring you. It might be fifteen days later, but he will absolutely do it.

SC: Everyone goes through changes. I think it's worth reflecting on the fact that perhaps you went through some as well. You would have to admit that sometimes you are a hard workmate. Of that there can be no doubt.

RH: Yes, I mean I can be.

SC: You must know that you can be very intimidating, and I think you've toned that down some in recent years.

RH: Yes, yes, I know what you're saying, but that's part of what I do to get my job done, and I don't really mean it. It's something I can turn on purely to get the job done. And you have to be like that in the music business to make things work for you. Because if you don't, people will just tread on you.

SC: You have a very strong sense of the "business" and I clearly remember you saying several times that it's important to remember that people in the "business" are not your friends, per se.

RH: You have to understand that you are doing a job, the same as everyone else, and the reality is they [bands] are not your friends. You are employed by them. You can have a good time with them. You can enjoy yourself with them, but you are not "them," which is something a lot of people who do this forget. You can go on tour with them, you can live in this strange, ethereal world that [most] people don't inhabit, a timeless world, really, but it's important to remember that it's their timeless world and not yours.

SC: Can personal feelings affect the way you see people through the lens?

RH: I've left that a long time [ago]. I'm employed to make someone look as good as I can in the time I have. And that is what I think I'm good at doing. Look, with Metallica I'd be a complete liar if I said I didn't love working for them. And if they stop using me now, I'd be really, really disappointed. I really would be upset. Because they're comfortable with me and I'm comfortable with them. We're older now. They let me do my thing. And one thing I'll say with them is that as long as they trust you, they will leave you to do things your way. I like that.

SC: What impact has digital photography had on your work?

RH: I think one of the problems with digital photography is it makes any idiot think they're a photographer. Because with a digital camera you can get a result, which with film you can't. Because film requires you to think more. And there's more to taking a photograph than people realize. They think they can just walk into a show with a digital camera and it's easy. It's not easy. You've still gotta know what you're doing and how to do it. Anyone can shoot eight thousand shots and get something, but you're still not going to even get ten really good shots unless you know what you're doing. I sometimes think digital photography in a sense has ruined the art of shooting.

SC: You're talking about the framing, composition . . .

RH: . . . yes. And also, any black-and-white you see of mine has been shot on film. I still use film. I'm pretty vehement about it, I still like shooting with Ilford film, I always will.

SC: What was the hardest shoot you've ever done with Metallica? The most difficult, biggest pain in the arse?

RH: One of them was on the *Live Shit* tour, when Kirk had that sort of "Rastafarian dreadlock" look, because they just couldn't be bothered. I was shooting them in Denver or Salt Lake or somewhere, and I got them to do it, but there was no interest doing it. And also, I think the first time I shot them in the studio in LA for a *Q* magazine cover [for the *Death Magnetic* album], it was part of a press day. And the studio stuff of the band was, I thought, disappointing. They were really not into it, and they just wanted to get it over with. I stayed on after and shot James and Kirk, and that was easy. I prefer the ones I did a few days later in Tucson with just them hanging backstage. They were far more into it and far more informal. But look, it's not always easy and it's not always loads of fun; a lot of times it is—we recently shot in Mexico City and had a great time at the pyramids—but the most important thing is to do the job and do it properly. Which is one thing over the years we have worked together that I think has always, undeniably happened. And that result takes both parties being on the same page to make it work. So really, when I look back at all of this, it seems pretty clear that we've been on the same page a lot of times!

SC: It would be remiss if I did not also ask you about your assistants through the years, the people who schlep impossibly heavy bags, produce lenses and film for you at lightning speed, and who show Zen levels of patience.

RH: Well, in my world, I just want to be able to concentrate on what I do, which is taking photos. And in that sense, at a gig it's nice to have some-one make sure no one is flying through the air about to land on my back! But the other thing is, you do often need equipment very, very quickly; you need film, lenses, whatever, to be right there. And if you spend time doing that, then you have a band standing around getting disgruntled or you miss a great moment live, so an assistant is very important. And I've been lucky with the people I've used, because they know almost telepathically the lenses

I want, the camera I want, what settings I want, and the lighting I want set up when I use a setup situation requiring lights. Going through them, there was Rory Moles, who was good at lighting but found the band far beneath him—he now works on films. He had actually been suggested to me by Andrew Clatworthy, whom I met at Holborn Studios in London. He enjoyed the job, was good at reading my mind, and was a very hard worker. Andrew also once said there were three types of angry with me:

1. Tired and jetlagged
2. Annoyed but not mad
3. Really angry, and you are usually right.

And he also said that whenever I'd been an arsehole I would always apologize, which is true so far as I'm concerned. Laurence Baker was more of a friend, who is now a photographer and shoots a lot of motor racing. He was "The Naked Man" because with every band I shot that he helped with, he would pretend to go and get something while taking his clothes off and sneaking up behind the band! I have a photo of Jason Newsted passed out with Laurence's balls in his hair while Lars, James, and Kirk grin inanely next to him . . . and no, it's not for this book! Noriaki Watanabe, also known as General Noriega, is my right-hand man . . . which is pretty good considering he has no right hand. I met him at the first Metallica show in Japan, in 1986, and I liked his "way." The General only

has one arm, one eye, and thirty percent hearing out of one ear, yet he can read my mind better than anyone and is always ready to serve "the Master"! And I hate to admit I couldn't function without Kazuyo Horie (okay, I could, but it would be hard). Kaz was a student who was living at my Mum's house but ended up never going home; she's now Irish with a full Irish passport. . . . It's amazing what you can get away with! Kaz knows how I want a photo to look, and I mean knows *exactly*, she does all of my digital work, looks after my negatives, my digital files, all of it, really. In fact if I need to show, say, James a photo, I'll let her pick it, as she knows what he wants. I seriously thank them all, I should thank Kaz for her continual efforts, and a big thank-you to Noriaki for putting my whole Metallica file in order and helping with the choice of photographs for this book.

SC: I have to ask one more thing in bringing this to a close; to paraphrase Clint Eastwood, "Do ya feel lucky? Well, do ya, punk?"

RH: I like to think I make it look easy, but it isn't. It actually makes me laugh a lot when people say, "Well, lucky for you, you do Metallica." What they don't get is the hard work I've put in. I think I helped make Metallica look the way they are, image-wise. Some people think you just turn up and it's just "Hey, presto, it all happens and it's really easy." It is not easy. Believe me, it's not.

A bit like mustard, sour on its own, okay with company . . . hmmm . . . is that being too nice???

He does takes the best live shots in the world, and can be a nice guy when you water him regularly. The first time I met him I didn't think people like him actually existed outside of books and movies (e.g., Ebenezer Scrooge), but I wasn't as worldly as I am now. Never make a business transaction with him, because you'll feel like a cheap prostitute who just turned a trick with the guy in the "One" video.

He can be amazingly nice and compassionate sometimes, but usually after a few vodkas . . .

The worst thing about Ross is that his god-awful qualities have a way of rubbing off on you after a while, like farting in public, insulting impulsively, and having a general disregard for anything and everything in earshot. . . .

. . . So why do I like the guy so much? Because he is honest, has artistic integrity, and can be an amazingly loyal friend, especially when he NEEDS to. He has an eye and a view like none of the other rock photographers do in the heat of the live performance, not afraid to straddle the stage and get in the way, and always a good sport about MOST things. I think the reason he was so pissed off at us in the mid-nineties is not because we didn't use his services, but because he didn't get to hang out with us and share in all the good times and debauchery that was going on then; can't say I blame him!!!

ROSS HALFIN
PHOTOGRAPHY

A LETTER FROM A FAN.......

From: �█████████
Date: 6 April 2009 07:47:50 BST
To: ross@rosshalfin.com
Subject: YOUR A Greedy FUCKING WANKER !! YOU STUCK UP CUNT !!

HEY ASSHOLE !!
I encountered your sorry ass at the METALLICA party the other night & I must say I was
shocked & saddened by your very UNPROFESSIONAL behavior !!
I was also "ATTEMPTING" to photograph the evening & you were a FUCKING
ASSHOLE !!! (But you already know that !!)

YOU CAME EXTREMELY CLOSE TO HAVING yer HUGE BULBOUS suntanned
NOGGIN beat to a bloody pulp !! I did not proceed cause I am a gentleman !!

Contrary to what you might believe...you DID NOT have the exclusive that night !!
You have toured with the band extensively thru the years & have FUCKING MILLIONS
of shots of the guys..I am blown away by how self centered & GREEDY you are !!
You're like an annoying little puppy following Mr.Page around like a teenage fanboy !!
He is truly a classy British gentleman where as you give the entire BRITISH a
HORRIBLE REP !!

Your WHINING diary piece in SO WHAT really showed yer true colors !!
How dare you insult ROBB FLYNN of the TRULY LEGENDARY Machine Head..
Yeah right.. like he's an asshole for taking "PRECIOUS TIME" away from your shoot
with Lars !!
Gimme a FUCKING BREAK !!

You are the EXTREME epitome of POMPOUS BRITISH WANKERY & a huge TURD
who gives ROCK PHOTOGRAPHERS a BAD NAME all over the world with yer
childish sniveleing rants & ego-"testicle" demeanor !!

It was hilarious to see you frantically trying to stop others from shooting from the crowd
& you came across like a complete & utter IDIOT !!

I sincerely hope you have a coronary from your stressed out life & ROT IN HELL for all
eternity !!

I'm pretty easygoing & I get along well with everybody & I'm sure you don't give a flying
FUCK what I or anyone else thinks about you ..

However... mark my words MR. Halfwit !! Your time will come !!
I am a firm believer in KARMA & one day very soon you will get yer come-uppance !!
You are a very sad person who is despised by 100's of yer colleagues & you will
eventually die a pathetic lonely old FUCK !!

I met you backstage at a MAIDEN show a long time ago & I looked up to you as an
aspiring fotographer..You could not have been more of a jerk to me then & also were a
TOTAL FOOKIN'prick at misc Metallica gigs thru the
years !!

I sincerely hope you keel over from a heart attack TODAY & get what you deserve for
being the shittiest GREEDY piece of excrement I have ever had the displeasure of
meeting !!

Thanks for yer time & have an awful day you worthless FUCK !!

LOVE, a disgruntled fellow fotographer !!

PS I'm sure your too much of a pussy to respond to this...So go ahead & file this away
with the rest of yer HUGE HATEMAIL FILE !!

FUCK OFF & DIE YOU SACK OF SHIT !!!!